SOLAR POWER

Published by Smart Apple Media

1980 Lookout Drive

North Mankato, Minnesota 56003

Design and Production by EvansDay Design

Photographs: Richard Cummins, Image Finders
(Mark Gibson, Dave Haas, Jo Williams), JLM Visuals
(Breck Kent), Robert McCaw, Tom Myers

LIBRARY OF CONGRESS CATALOGING-IN-PUBLICATION DATA

Gibson, Diane, 1966–

Solar power / by Diane Gibson.

p. cm. — (Sources of energy)

Includes index.

Summary: Describes the use of solar power since
early times, the science which explains how solar
power works, and its advantages and disadvantages.
Includes a simple experiment.

ISBN 1-887068-78-3

1. Solar energy—Juvenile literature. [1. Solar energy.]
I. Title. II. Series.

TJ810.3 .G53   2000

621.47—dc21   99-036196

FIRST EDITION

9 8 7 6 5 4 3 2 1

solarpower

DIANE GIBSON

solarpower

THE SUN IS A GIANT BALL OF BURNING GASES 93 MILLION MILES (1.5 MILLION KM) FROM EARTH. ITS HEAT AND LIGHT TRAVEL SO FAST THAT THEY TAKE ONLY ABOUT EIGHT MINUTES TO REACH OUR PLAN-ET. THE HEAT AND LIGHT FROM THE SUN ARE KNOWN AS SOLAR ENERGY. WITHOUT THE SUN'S ENERGY, NO PLANTS, ANIMALS, OR PEOPLE COULD LIVE ON EARTH. OUR PLANET WOULD BE NOTHING BUT AN ICY ROCK FLOATING IN SPACE.

SOLAR PANELS

⊙ SOME PEOPLE USE solar panels to heat their homes. Solar panels are thin, rectangular boxes that are usually built on the roof of a house. Because dark colors attract heat better than light colors, the panels are painted a dull black. Inside each panel is air or water that is heated as the panel sits in the sun. Once it is warm enough, the air or water is moved through the house.   ◈   The heated air or water can be moved in different ways. Machines, such as fans and pumps, are often used to spread warm air around the house. Gravity, the force that draws objects toward the earth, is often used to move heated water. Gravity pulls the water from the panel down a pipe and into a storage tank. Fans may then spread air warmed by the water, or pumps may send the water directly to faucets in the house.   ◈   Some solar panels are placed on the ground up against the house. The panels help to warm the air in a space under the house. Since heated air is lighter than cold air, it rises up through the floor to keep the inside of the house warm.

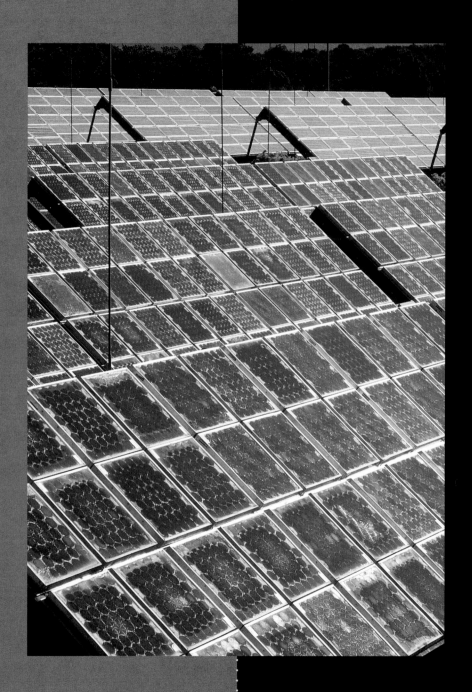

SOLAR PANELS ABSORB THE
SUN'S ENERGY, ALLOWING
PEOPLE TO CAPTURE AND
USE ITS HEAT.

BECAUSE THEY USE
MAINLY SOLAR ENERGY,
SPACE SHUTTLES DON'T
HAVE TO CARRY A LOT
OF HEAVY FUEL.

Greenhouses are buildings that keep plants warm in the winter. They have clear roofs that let in the sun's energy then trap the heat. NASA has been using solar energy to power its spacecraft since 1958. In fact, most of the electricity used by space shuttles in orbit comes from the sun.

GREENHOUSES LET IN SUNLIGHT AND TRAP ITS HEAT, ALLOWING PLANTS TO GROW EVEN IN COLD REGIONS.

Photovoltaic (solar) cells gather the energy that solar-powered vehicles need to run.

SOLAR CELLS

⊙ THE SUN'S POWER can also be used to produce **electricity**. A different kind of solar panel is used to do this; it is long and flat and covered with **photovoltaic** cells called solar cells. These cells are shaped like pancakes and are made from silicon, a type of mineral found in sand. The silicon changes the energy in sunlight into electric power. Wires connect the cells to a battery so the electricity can be stored and used later. ◎ Scientists have built cars and airplanes that run on solar energy. These machines are covered with solar cells to collect the sun's energy. They also include **batteries** to store the energy. So far none of these machines have been able to travel very far—especially in cloudy weather. Building solar-powered cars and planes is tricky, since they must be big enough to hold all the cells they need, yet small and light enough to move easily. Scientists hope to soon design solar-powered vehicles that will be available to people everywhere.

THE ENERGY RE-
LEASED BY THE SUN IS
MORE THAN ENOUGH · · ·
TO MEET THE NEEDS
OF THE WORLD.

In 1981, the English Channel was crossed by a solar-powered airplane called *Solar Challenger*. The first solar panel was built in 1908 by William J. Bailey in California.

In 40 minutes, the earth receives enough solar energy to power all of the world's machines for one year. But we are able to harness only a fraction of this power.

In ALBUQUERQUE, NEW MEXICO, is a solar power station called a "power tower." This unique station was built as a test to see how well it could create electricity from the sun's energy. The tower stands 200 feet (61 m) high and holds 1,775 mirrors that **reflect** sunlight to a point at the very top of the tower. The heat collected by the tower causes a pool of water to boil, producing steam. The steam is used to power machines called generators, which create electricity.   During the 1960s, a solar furnace was built in Odeillo, France. A solar furnace is also a type of power tower, only it collects sunlight with small, flat mirrors placed on a hillside. As the sun moves across the sky, these mirrors also move so that they are always collecting its light. The mirrors reflect the sunlight to another larger wall of mirrors, which is 133 feet (40 m) high and 165 feet (50 m) wide.   All of these mirrors point to one place on a tower

POWER TOWERS USE AN ARRAY OF MIRRORS TO CONCENTRATE SUNLIGHT ON THE TOWER'S FOCAL POINT.

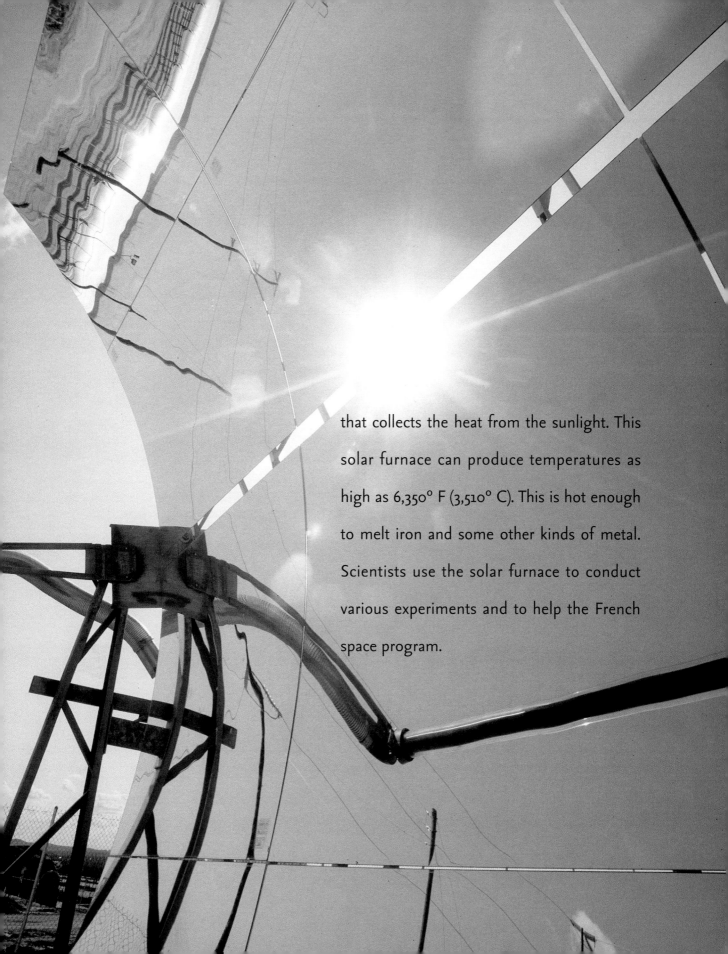

that collects the heat from the sunlight. This solar furnace can produce temperatures as high as 6,350° F (3,510° C). This is hot enough to melt iron and some other kinds of metal. Scientists use the solar furnace to conduct various experiments and to help the French space program.

SOLAR ENERGY CAN POWER A WIDE VARI-ETY OF MACHINES AND FACILITIES, INCLUDING LIGHTHOUSES.

Solar Two, a power tower built in 1996 in California, can create enough electricity on a sunny day to meet the daily needs of up to 10,000 people.

The first solar cells were made in 1889 by American inventor Charles Fritts. They were very small—only about the size of a quarter. In 1874, the world's largest solar still was built in Chile. It could produce 6,000 gallons (22,700 l) of drinking water every day, and did so for 40 years.

FIELDS OF MIRRORS CALLED HELIOSTATS ARE USED TO COLLECT SOLAR ENERGY FOR POWER STATIONS.

THE FUTURE OF SOLAR POWER

◉ ONE DRAWBACK TO using solar power is that the sun allows us to make the most electricity when we need it the least—during the day. Also, all of the panels and mirrors required for solar power stations are very expensive to buy and can take up a lot of space. ◎ Scientists and engineers continue to look for better and cheaper ways to collect and use the sun's energy. Much of the energy in the world today is produced by burning fuels such as coal and oil. Unfortunately, burning fuels release dangerous poisons into the air. Also, the earth has a limited amount of coal and oil. Once it's used up, there's nowhere else to get more. ◎ Solar power is clean and safe for the environment. No dangerous chemicals are released into the air, and—as long as the sun shines—it is an unlimited supply of energy. Once we learn to better harness the sun's power, the world may get most of its electricity from that great burning ball in the sky.

POWER TOWERS ARE USU-
ALLY BUILT IN WARM AREAS
WHERE THE SUN SHINES
BRIGHTLY YEAR-ROUND.

MACHINES THAT ARE FUELED BY THE SUN'S POWER DO NOT POL- LUTE THE AIR OR ENVIRONMENT.

During the 1870s, a newspaper in France was printed with the help of solar power. It was called *The Sun Journal.*

⊙ PEOPLE HAVE BEEN using solar energy for thousands of years. Ancient Greeks learned to start fires with it. They reflected sunlight off a shiny piece of metal onto dried grass or twigs until the dry material got hot enough to burn. Early Native Americans knew that the winter sun was mostly in the southern half of the sky. And since it shined in the west during the afternoon, they built their homes to face southwest. Many homes were built with adobe, which is sun-dried clay. The adobe collected the sun's heat during the day and released it at night, keeping the people inside warm. Today, many houses are still built facing the sun.

HUMANS LEARNED LONG AGO THAT ADOBE IS AN EFFECTIVE MATERIAL FOR TRAPPING THE SUN'S HEAT.

◉ **Building A Solar Still** Solar energy can be used to turn saltwater into drinking water. You can make a solar still at home. You will need:

A metal pot	**A tablespoon**
A heavy cup	**Salt**
Water	**Plastic food wrap**
Tape	**A small rock**

◉ Fill the pot with an inch (2.5 cm) of water. Stir a tablespoon (15 ml) of salt into the water. Place the cup in the middle of the pot. It should be heavy enough that it doesn't float. The cup should not be higher than the sides of the pot.

◉ Cover the pot with plastic food wrap and tape the sides so no air can get in or out. Carefully set the rock directly over the cup. The rock should make the wrapping sag a little but shouldn't touch the cup. Now set your still in bright sunshine.

◉ The heat from the sun will warm the water and slowly turn it into steam. The steam will cool on the wrapping and form into tiny drops of water that roll toward the rock and fall into the cup. The water in the cup will be salt-free and good to drink.

Batteries ARE CONTAINERS FILLED WITH CHEMI-CALS THAT CAN PRODUCE OR STORE ELECTRICAL POWER.

Electricity IS A TYPE OF ENERGY USED IN HOMES TO RUN LIGHTS AND APPLIANCES.

NASA IS A SHORTENED NAME FOR THE NATIONAL AERONAUTICS AND SPACE ADMINISTRATION.

A **photovoltaic** OBJECT IS ONE THAT GENERATES ELECTRICITY WHEN STRUCK BY RADIATION ENERGY.

TO **reflect** LIGHT IS TO BOUNCE IT OFF AN OBJECT.